Network Marketing 101
Ultimate Guide to Create Passive Income from MLM Business

Danny Richmond

Text Copyright © [Danny Richmond]

All rights reserved. No part of this guide may be reproduced in any form without permission in writing from the publisher except in the case of brief quotations embodied in critical articles or reviews.

Legal & Disclaimer

The information contained in this book and its contents is not designed to replace or take the place of any form of medical or professional advice; and is not meant to replace the need for independent medical, financial, legal or other professional advice or services, as may be required. The content and information in this book have been provided for educational and entertainment purposes only.

The content and information contained in this book have been compiled from sources deemed reliable, and it is accurate to the best of the Author's knowledge, information, and belief. However, the Author cannot guarantee its accuracy and validity and cannot be held liable for any errors and/or omissions. Further, changes are periodically made to this book as and when needed. Where appropriate and/or necessary, you must consult a professional (including but not limited to your doctor, attorney, financial advisor or such other professional advisor) before using any of the suggested remedies, techniques, or information in this book.

Upon using the contents and information contained in this book, you agree to hold harmless the Author from and against any damages, costs, and expenses, including any legal fees potentially resulting from the application of any of the information provided by this book. This disclaimer applies to any loss, damages or injury caused by the use and application, whether directly or indirectly, of any advice or information presented, whether for breach of contract, tort, negligence, personal injury, criminal intent, or under any other cause of action.

You agree to accept all risks of using the information presented inside this book.

You agree that by continuing to read this book, where appropriate and/or necessary, you shall consult a professional (including but not limited to your doctor, attorney, or financial advisor or such other advisor as needed) before using any of the suggested remedies, techniques, or information in this book.

Table of Contents

Contents

Introduction 4

Chapter 1 – Traditional Marketing Vs. Network Marketing: What is the Real Difference? 5

Chapter 2 – Benefits of Network Marketing 7

Chapter 3 – Is Success in Network Marketing Luck or Skill? 10

Chapter 4 – Getting Started: Essential Marketing Tools to Jumpstart your Network Marketing Business 12

Chapter 5 – Common Mistakes People Make at Network Marketing 15

Chapter 6 – The Importance of "Networking" in your Networking Marketing Business 18

Chapter 7 – Tips for a Successful Network Marketing Business 20

Conclusion 22

Also, Check Out This Other Book Published by Success Publishing 23

Free Preview Bonus 24

Introduction

Job opportunities, careers, ministry, and vocations are all ways of people to search for personal fulfillment. These are productive activities where we will be able to apply interest and passion to our talents. In today's society, the purpose of being dedicated to a career, job, or vocation was misrepresented. It is a normal response that their choice or reason was because of money when that are asked about a certain job or career.

People who propel their lives with this ideology find a void in their lives. Money is a great way of measuring how you generate to the society by offering solutions to their problems, while also building communities of those dedicated experts. Money is only a tool that you can use to measure how much value you bring to people's lives. In business, value can be generated for your clients by offering them solutions to their problems while building communities of dedicated professionals.

You can easily see why business owners are making lots of money. This is because they are bringing much value to the people around them. Providing solution to the problem of dissatisfaction and discomfort with your career or job might be as simple as having to redefine what you do. You may also look for personal fulfillment in something else. However, there is one common mistake that people do when they search for professional fulfillment, and it is self-employment.

When you become self-employed, you will be your own manager, customer service, accountant, loss prevention, sales department, labor, and attorney. People go in business because they love to offer value and service to others. It is not necessarily because they love all the involved paperwork with it. The good news is that there is a solution for people who want to find personal fulfillment that does not require having to invest in purchasing, operating, or starting a traditional business.

The solution will help you focus your energy and time on what is most important, which is to generate value for people without worrying about all the overhead. This solution is network marketing and it has helped millions in different forms.

Chapter 1 – Traditional Marketing Vs. Network Marketing: What is the Real Difference?

Are you looking for a better way to generate great amount of money to your bank account, ways that will allow you to collect prospects without having any hassle at all? What if there has been a way to do this? What if there has been a way to get your team a prospect effectively and earn money, without a need to use traditional methods that almost wiped out the people's belief in you, together with your amazing opportunity?

A traditional company typically have a Vice President of Marketing with many regional managers who would report to them directly. These regional managers will be recruiting, hiring, training, and managing area managers who would, in turn, also be recruiting, hiring, training, and managing sales representatives. Then, the sales representatives will be the ones responsible for selling the products and services of company.

In line with this, the shape of a traditional company would look like a pyramid or triangle. It is somewhat obvious that the higher the level, the higher the pay and there would be less room at the top for advancement. Also, it has been evident that mathematically, it is not possible for every sales representative or for an employee to rise to the top no matter how good job they do.

Network marketing is different. Every individual begins exactly in the same level, at the top of their own company. They have the same opportunity as everyone else, and they are compensated in direct proportion to the success or activity that they have had an influence in generation. Another thing about network marketing is that there is no need to be a sales representative to reap the level of financial benefits that company owners, marketers, and sales managers associated to them.

As contrary to traditional companies, you will only need to work with, for, and when you want. You work for yourself and for those whose activity generates income for you. You can even choose to work with people whom you generate income for because they do not make money unless you do.

Product Distribution Ways

In traditional marketing, when customers buy a product or service from a retailer, the money will be divided to four different sectors of supply chain, within the manufacturer, wholesaler, distributor, and retailer, and then to customer. However, the profit chain here is shorter, which is divided to customer, manufacturer, and distributor.

Advertising

These days, customers are very skeptical and they experience an information overload. It results to ignoring the expensive TV advertisements and print ads created by marketing team. On the other hand, they are asking for recommendation from people around, including family, relatives, neighbors, friends, co-workers, or other people with any experience in the product that they need. Then, invisible marketing will be created.

It is always recognized by companies that the power of word-of-mouth is superior, and they believe that it is much more effective as compared to advertisement created by the seller. This kind of recommendation is also referred to as viral marketing or word-of-mouth advertising, and it recently gets more indicative term – buzz.

When you purchase a service or product, you are either performing independent research about the product, or asking for recommendations. You can easily get information because people like talking about themselves and their experiences in like. They like sharing and recommending. People recommend everything, including products and services that they use and satisfied with. These products may include phone they use, phone services, car they drive, or car services that they are using.

They even recommend where to take vacation and which movie to see. This list can go on and on, and it has been the most powerful marketing strategy. Even though it is used in traditional marketing broadly; in network marketing companies, the product will move only through the word-of-mouth marketing.

Chapter 2 – Benefits of Network Marketing

Network marketing has developed into a billion-dollar industry since its humble beginnings in year 1950. Without regards to their color, race, nationality, creed, or economic situation, network marketing is offering the opportunity to attain their dreams through a path that is meant to provide the financial means and personal growth for an equal platform for everyone. Here are the benefits of network marketing to promote your opportunity and recruit partners in your company.

1. **Little amount of risk**

    There is a amount of inherited risk involved when you become a small business owner or an entrepreneur. We are mostly confronted with wasting time, losing money, and not being profitable right away, among others. In a traditional company, the associated cost with starting up and opening your business is what holds people back to become the creators of their own destiny. People do not like risk and they are trying to avoid it at all costs.

    You would like a guarantee and you are inclined to maintain your comfort zones. In business, you will not be able to eliminate the risks, but you can learn to minimize them. The advantage of starting a network marketing business is that you will have minimal risk. Commonly, if you several hundred dollars, you can get started with a company that you want. You can even market the products and services that you might be consuming already. The financial commitment is not necessary as compared to that of a traditional company, which diminish even more drastically in comparison to possible return on investment.

2. **Income potential**

    You will not have any cap on how much money you are generating. In the corporate jobs, the big limitation is that no matter how hard your work for these companies, your income is tethered to a market standard for someone who has your skills. The network marketing industry has produced more millionaires of average people as compared to other industries.

    With network marketing, you have all the privilege to decide on how much you want to earn. A network marketing company will not hold you back in the same way that the corporate environment does. They are not actually incentivizing your wealth creation and increased productivity. If you have the skill sets of a trained network marketer, you are capable of making any income you want, based on your dedication, persistence, drive, willingness, and diligence to help others. Nevertheless, these skills are the key. As soon as you have trained yourself to become a marketer, you will be able to market anything you want and you can generate the income you seek.

3. **Leverage**

   Your network marketing business is a scalable business, people business, duplicable system, a business that exponentially increases personal productivity, and a business of teamwork and synergy. There are unspeakable rewards that you can reap by leveraging the efforts of the people you help. This will develop a collective mindset, promoting a win-win relationship. It is a business model with elegance because everyone will be able to share in the same fortune and lifestyle as those over them.

4. **No inventory to carry**

   Traditional companies would have distributors stack up on the inventory, and this concept alone gave a bad rap to the industry for years. However, network marketing is capitalizing on the tools and technology available. They have high-speed internet, web conferencing, internet telephony, teleconferencing, automated customer relationship management systems, and auto shipping or drop shipping. Not maintaining your product inventory can make your business more agile in the market condition.

5. **Great demand for good quality products or services**

   There are many network marketing companies representing superior quality products and services. When considering a company that you want to get involved with, you may ask yourself if you are going to consume those products or services if you are not selling them, or if you are bringing value to your clients when they consume your products and services.

   Other things that you would ask are if your products or services are faddish, if your products or services bring any benefit to your customers in addition to an opportunity to make money, and about how vulnerable your products and services are to a changing economy. All businesses need and want repeat customers. Distributors will be paid only when they have customers for their products, and if their customers continue that consumption. That makes a continually growing income stream.

6. **Attainable freedom**

   When you have a productive business in network marketing, you are provided with lifestyle to you that only the famous and rich people enjoyed. However, it can be fulfilled when all the pieces are in place. It is the dream that all new distributors want to realize, and you can only attain it when there is a clear understanding about how you can get there and about when your marketing skills would be sharp. Hence, this is not just about money, but about the fulfilling dreams and attaining highest quality of life that makes a network marketing business the best business to engage.

7. **No employees to hire**

   It is by far the among the clearest advantage of networking marketing as compared to traditional businesses. A network marketing company is a business of people who work together interdependently. Even if you do not have any employees, you can build a business right from home. It is an industry that provides additional benefit of being in business without the employee's excuses, negative dispositions, concerns, excuses, and more. With a network of independent business owners who work together into a common goal, you will be able to attain the results of major corporations with no headaches and overhead.

8. **Residual income**

   You are paying your electric bill, gas, and phone bill monthly. These are the kinds of services that provide your ongoing residual income stream. The greatest benefit of considering a network marketing business is that it brings you the opportunity of enjoying residual income just as that of the major companies. If you can do one thing one time, and then, get paid repeatedly for that one thing, you have residual income. If you need to continue selling products and services to make or maintain your income, you have brought another job to yourself. You are used to trading your time for wages that you most commonly don't see or understand the power and concept of residual income, but it is the thing that makes a viable network marketing opportunity for you.

9. **Portability**

   Through technological advancement, you will be able to do what distributors cannot do decades ago, and that's what makes network marketing portable. There is now phone technology that enables you to take your phone and move it anywhere you like, which is transparent to your clients, partners, and prospects. With just an access to the internet, you can take calls on computer, laptop, or your phone, and continue to do business on the go, regardless if you are on vacation or visiting relatives in another city or country.

10. **Low operating costs**

    The network marketing model is what makes it possible to run a business at low cost. As compared to more traditional business models, network marketing has remained a more sensible selection unquestionable. This is where the support of your upline should come in. You can use the knowledge, expertise, and personal power of a good upline mentor, and they can help you in generating the funds to pay off your investments. Thus, you can get into profit even when you are just getting started.

Chapter 3 – Is Success in Network Marketing Luck or Skill?

Network marketing is among the most rapidly growing but also the most misunderstood method of moving products in use these days. It started in 1960 in the US and there are people, who see this industry as a resort for those who couldn't get a place in the traditional business industry. However, just as with any other product or service distribution model, network marketing is an honorable means hot business model and livelihood. It is important to understand what network marketing in order to correct the negative and uninformed knowledge planted in the minds of many people, who have been listening to people who are not able to wait to understand how this industry works before quitting on their network marketing business.

Network marketing means more than 1 level of network. There are 3 methods of moving products. One if retailing or wholesaling model. It is the traditional distribution model that uses the wholesaler and advertisement media for moving their products, and it has been the most common model. However, this method is aimed to enrich the rich advertisement agencies and wholesalers. Another method is direct sale, in which the service provider or manufacturer sells the product directly to the customer. Nevertheless, here, the sales are emphasized instead of sharing. The last method of moving products network marketing, wherein the service provider or manufacturer is offering their services or products directly to the customers at the cost price. These manufacturers or service providers will even pay compensation to customers for purchasing their products or services and for sharing it with their family, relatives, friends, and associates.

Most objections of people about network marketing are not being able to realize the difference between direct sales method of marketing and the network marketing. Network marketing is not necessarily about door-to-door selling of products, but about sharing valuable products and services. The most significant difference between direct sales and network marketing is that you will be in business for yourself in network marketing. On the other hand, in direct sales, you will not be for yourself only, but for the company that you represent. Rather, you will be buying the products in wholesale from the company you are representing. It means that you will be able to use those products for their own consumption.

Keep in mind that many people get involved in a company at the beginning because of this alone. Also, many people will get serious in building a business along the line. Because you purchase your products in wholesale, you may sell these products in a retail brand and make a profit. Among the most common misunderstanding about network marketing is the notion that you need to sell retail if you want to succeed. The most significant point is that you need to let your sales come as the natural result of building the organization. More and more people fail because they try doing it the other way around. One example is that they try building the company through the emphasis of selling.

The word "selling" has triggered negative thoughts in the minds of around 95% of people. In network marketing, there is no need to sell the products in the traditional sense of word. Nonetheless, products do not need to move to get paid. Selling means calling on strangers and trying to sell them something that they may not need, or even want. The economic value of a network is equal to the number of users squared. This means that if there is even just one phone, that single phone won't have any economic value. As soon as there comes 2 phones, the phone network's value will now be squared. This economic value will rise exponentially, and not numerically.

Alternately, in network marketing, when building an organization, you are building a network where you can channel your products. The foundation of network marketing is retailing. The sales in-network marketing come from members who share it with their friends, relative, family, and neighbors. They never need to talk to strangers but they are consciously making more friends and sharing their products with them. It requires skills and taking action to succeed in network marketing. Being mentored by someone who has attained success in the industry is among the quickest way of becoming successful in network marketing.

Chapter 4 – Getting Started: Essential Marketing Tools to Jumpstart your Network Marketing Business

There are necessary tools that you will need to help you in your network marketing business. It will help you attain new levels of success with your business. There are free tools and there are the paid ones. The good news is that there are free alternative tools available for the tools that do require money. You just have to look for them thoroughly.

- **Social networking**

    Social media websites exploded into something that have not been predicted. Without account on Twitter, Facebook, and MySpace, you miss out on the action. These are not only great tools to be used for socializing with family and friends, but also an incredible tool for network marketers. Social networking sites will help you connect with those whom you cannot connect with in the real world. Social networking is not about logging into Facebook and then, blast your business opportunity to your friends. It is a common mistake that many network marketers do. Social networking is very powerful if used in the right way.

- **Webinar hosting**

    The secret of network marketers who succeed is giving live webinar presentations. Webinar hosting does lots of things for your business. Being capable of hosting a webinar can change how you market to your list of prospects dramatically, while also establishing yourself as a leader within your company. There are many people who have been paid for hosting webinars.

- **Marketing campaign**

    Having a marketing campaign is important to any network marketer who wants to build their business online. Think of internet as a major interstate highway. There are millions, or even billions of people who travel online per second. But how many of them have knowledge about your business? How many of them have information about you? If you do not have a marketing campaign, it is very hard for people to know about your network marketing business and if they do, it will not be from you.

- **Innovative training**

    Training is among the most important network marketing tool that you cannot live without. The web continues to change and you will have to stay in front of the trend if you want to succeed in the industry. There is an innovation and strategy every day when it comes to marketing your business on the web, in which some online marketing beginners make millions of dollars when they use it. With the right training, you will be in the advantage, keeping you on track and on trends.

- **Blog**

Blog is a site acting as the central nervous system of the whole marketing campaign. Network marketing is a business necessitating people to network with others to be able to reach sales generation. Blogs are quite the same in nature. When you set up a blog, you are connecting all your websites together, including capture pages, articles, social networking, videos, company sites, and more, and form a web effect that your prospective customers will run into.

- **Capture pages**

You may scratch your head and wonder what does capture page means. It is a site that require the visitor to enter their contact information to proceed to the next page. An email and a name is most commonly what you are after. You can use capture pages to entice the visitor to subscribe or opt-in to your website so that they can continue on to more information. These are like TV commercials or billboards but they are better and more effective.

- **Article Marketing**

The power of article marketing has helped many network marketing business successful, providing a solution to their problem. When people search for a review of certain product in search engine like Google, they are planning to join or buy the product. If you write an article about a certain product, you can have thousands of prospects by reading your article. However, it takes time to have an effective article marketing, and it requires research. The good thing is that you can develop it through time.

- **Pay Per Click**

Pay Per Click is a paid type of advertising. The greater thing about it is that you will be able to set up a campaign for any budget that you may have. It can even be as low as $1 each day. If you do it in the right way, you can net a profit monthly. Even more benefit is that PPC helps your profit seal up to thousands of dollars per day. However, the necessary knowledge is the same.

- **Email Auto-Responder**

Email auto-responder helps you communicate with the contacts you get from capture pages in an effective way. You may set up automated emails and send it out every day to your list of contacts. Having the capability to communicate to your list of great importance and must not be ignored.

- **Screen recording**

    Video marketing is an important tool in network marketing. If you are not making videos to be posted online, you will lose much traffic. Perhaps the reason why you did not consider making videos is because you are not comfortable or you are too shy on a camera. You can use a screen recording tool to record your computer screen and save it as a video, without a need to show your face.

Chapter 5 – Common Mistakes People Make at Network Marketing

Network marketing is a business with no consistency. In this industry, some people are in wild success, with some being about to generate a modest income. However, most people dismally fail in network marketing and never make one sale. There are many common mistakes that people make when trying their hand at network marketing.

Lack of commitment

It takes great commitment to become successful in anything you do, and network marketing is no exception. There is a need to have commitment when you do something every day for the promotion of your business. This includes talking to people every day, and prospecting in order to find new people whom you should talk to. Another important thing in network marketing is to support those whom you already signed up into the business. Aside from that, you must spend some time to better get to know your product. Marketers who are successful in network marketing suggest spending time every day on business for at least 1-2 hrs. In line with this, it is important to commit on network marketing just as how you would on a conventional business. Your business will die if you are not committed.

Lack of belief in business model

Unless you totally believe in network marketing, it is highly recommended not to get involved. Network marketing is a tool that will help you in attaining an essential residual income while helping other people do the same. There are many, who have negative opinion about network marketing. This is because they see it as a pyramid selling, with the belief that the only ones who would make money are those who at the top of the pyramid. However, the truth is, network marketers at all levels will be able to make serious money. Marketers who are most successful are the ones who believe in the system and help others to become as successful as they do.

Lack of Team Support

Among the greatest mistake that people do in network marketing is because of a lack of team support. Unfortunately, there are many cases that as soon as someone signed up to a certain business, it will be the last thing that they would hear from their sponsor, so they need to do it effectively on their own. Many times, beginners in network marketing is handed with a manual, together with a pile of product and then, they are sent on their way, without any idea about the next step. Nonetheless, when you have a good leadership and team support, beginners in network marketing will have a bigger to become successful because they have someone who could encourage him and he will have people to help answer questions from the prospects.

Lack of belief in self

Another common mistake that network marketers do is not believing. They think they cannot sell. They do not totally believe that they have what it takes to attain success, or for that matter, they do not feel that they are rightful for success. However, the truth is that all of us have a right to succeed, and regardless if someone wants to admit it or not, all of us are in sale. Regardless if we are a computer engineer, a school teacher, or accountant, all of us are in sales. Each day, we try selling our opinions, ideas, and thoughts to other people. You may say that the words "influence" and "sales" can be interchanged. Believing in yourself is very important if you want to attain success not just in network marketing, but also in general life.

Lack of belief in the product

If you want to become successful in network marketing, you need to believe in the product you are promoting. It is among the obvious points, but this is one that many people get wrong the most. Believing in the product that you are promoting is important because it will come through when you talk about it to people. In addition, you are going to have more motivation to learn all you can about your product line, which helps you when you come promoting it.

Selling to the wrong people

Most commonly, because we are eager to get going in network marketing, we are trying to promote our business model and products to just anyone who comes our way. Also, in many cases, we have been hounding the wrong people. You will see that either someone is ready for your business or product, or they are not. You must be able to determine both. Stop spending your precious time trying to convince people who are interested in your business, and just focus your time to look for the hungry market. Also, you will find people who are still not ready. They are the ones you want to keep in touch with. Feed these people with the occasional piece of information and just be friends with them, because they know what you sell and promote, and they will let you know when they are ready.

Knowing what you sell

In network marketing, you are not selling the physical product, though it is what commonly help your clients to get initial interest from prospects. Rather, you are promoting an opportunity to make money. The entire concept of network marketing is building a network of business, and you will benefit when you help your prospects and clients to become success in their business. It is not the product that makes you money, but the promotion of business.

Becoming shy when bitten

Most probably, the greatest reason why people are struggling in network marketing is being afraid of rejection. They are scared to hear a big NO. Every NO is bringing you one step closer to a YES. However, this idea is not helpful to those who are scared to be rejected. The truth is that people do not reject you. They just say NO to your business opportunity or product. Successful marketers learn to adopt their NO as a vitamin. They learn from these lessons and there are many times that they can ask their prospects why they said NO. This can be a valuable information or lesson. It can help you when facing your next prospect. Also, it can help you understand that they do not reject you.

Wrong marketing methods

There are different people who like marketing their business and product in different ways. You may use internet marketing to promote your business. You can also talk to friends and family or use some kinds of advertising. You can have a different bent. The point is that you should find out what works for you and focus on that. In the same manner, you can try different marketing methods to find what brings you the best results.

There are many mistakes people do, which drive them to fail in network marketing, and it is a good place to start focusing on and start turning your own network marketing business around.

Chapter 6 – The Importance of "Networking" in your Networking Marketing Business

Having a complete understanding of the importance of network is a trait of successful marketers. While there are similarities between marketing and networking, you should come to a realization these are 2 not identical concepts. Both marketing and networking share a great reliance on interpersonal relations, and hence, they force people to overcome and confront the associated fears when they talk to other people. The potential of reject is present in both networking and marketing. Nevertheless, it has been countered by a wide opportunity for personal gain. For many, these words are dirty words.

Generally, it is a flawed understanding of the principles of networking that cause some to have resistance to the concept. It is a resistance that is very likely to be found in people who have belief that this industry is beneath their social status. Many see networking as a form of connection, simply to gain personal benefit. Those who are espousing this viewpoint can see networking to be shady, or not professional. This line of thinking has been rooted assuming that advancement only comes at the expense of other people.

Those who hold to this point of view regard life success as a proposition with zero sum. Adhering to this point of view will also shape your thinking about the field of network marketing. The idea of receiving personal gain from the efforts of other people is viewed in a negative light and considered inequitable. Successful marketers are fast in pointing out that their business was not built at the expense of others. As a matter of fact, the business of network marketing will reward people when helping others to attain success. From this point, the business model in network marketing could actually be among the fairest and most non-discriminating models that people use these days.

A successful network marketer is operating his business like a farmer and invest substantial amount of time to establish and nurture the interpersonal relationships. The common traits that you can find in successful network marketing include motivation, empowering, and equipping their business team, and investing in their network regularly. They will be able to leverage the synergy of their network without a need to take advantage of the team members inside the network.

In fact, both are regarded and recognized by those in the team. True professionals in network marketing strive to keep others' interest in their rightful position. This is an attention to personal care that makes working with a true professional very satisfying. Even though network marketing has lots of difference when compared to traditional business models, the importance of networking is just as important. It would be a mistake to underestimate how important is good networking skills, even when you utilize a business model aside from network marketing.

For people who really want to develop this skill, there are training and mentoring that come from marketers who built strong business organizations. Take time to connect with several people, who fit that description, tapping into their wisdom regarding this aspect of their life.

Chapter 7 – Tips for a Successful Network Marketing Business

Network marketing is effective, powerful, and it may explode your business. So, what is network marketing business. Knowing some tips will help you succeed in network marketing business.

1. **Building your mail list**

   You can use autoresponder software to start generating leads for your business. When you take time to put your contact details into your opt-in box, you know that they are interested in learning more. You can continue sending them follow-up emails, training, and tips through your autoresponder so that you can build relationship with them. When you build a substantial list, you have the chance to recruit people into your business while continuously building trust with them.

2. **Setting up a blog**

   This will be your headquarters online. This is where you distribute and craft all the content that you are making online. You can use a self-hosted blog. On the other hand, if you are a serious network marketer, getting a domain and hosting through web hosting service is the best move. It is not expensive, and it is customizable and professional. You may build your blog any way you like. Blog is the best way to be found on Google and other search engines. It is the best way of building an interactive community of people who share similar interest. Also, it is very easy to integrate with social media, and it has the capability of making your blog viral for even more traffic.

3. **Driving traffic to your content**

   When sharing the content that you create, you can use forums, social media sites, and other sites to drive traffic to your blog. You may share your links on Twitter, Facebook, and some social bookmarking websites. Start to follow people in your niche, who share the same interest as you, so you can start to drive them to your website.

4. **Creating quality content**

   What challenges are you facing when trying to get traffic, make sales, or generate leads. What do you want to learn as a marketer building your business on the web? What tips and strategies have you learned that you know other marketers would love getting their hands on, to start seeing their desired results. If you would be able to stay tuned to what people must know, together with the solutions that they want to find, you are going to be a valuable asset not just to your business, but also to others.

For instance, among the greatest challenges of building a network marketing business is about how to generate leads. Learn to overcome the lack of leads and share what you have learn on your blog. By helping other marketers to solve this problem, you will become an authority on the topic and you will start attracting people who want to learn from you and be partner with you in business.

5. **Being consistent**

Perhaps the most important if you want to become successful in this venture is being consistent. Many times, people quit before their breakthrough in their business. This is because they do not have consistency in their everyday marketing routine. They do not see the massive results that they see or expect others and so they give up too easily. When you have consistency, you have dedication to the entire process of building a successful business on the web. Meaning, it takes hard work, time, and simple implementation. Building a network marketing business has never been easy, but it is simple. Stay on the course and rewards are going to be more than you could have imagined.

Conclusion

Network marketing will continue growing and flourishing as more product companies find that leveraging people and their relationships in a share of profit is the best way of establishing their brand, more particularly because of the availability of social media, which has refined free advertising. As a manufacturer, would you pay a million dollars in advertising and media to get a chance to get customers? Or would you pay a commission for each sold product without a need to gamble with your money? This is the reason why network marketing has been very attractive to many businesses.

Not all network marketing companies would offer the same opportunity to you. There are some who offer massive bonus when they recruit and sell you the dream of having enough residual volume in your company one day and can receive a worthy retirement. Network marketing companies that serve this model are those offering energy or telecom services. The reason why most marketers in those industries do not make money is because there is a little residual paid out. Additionally, to be qualified for that little percentage will be tough in those companies.

The most profitable companies are offering environment and personal development and this will allow you to succeed, possibly not in network marketing company that you are in but within the interaction with those who are involved in your company. In line with this, you become a more effective, and professional person. It takes years to build and grow with those in your organization. The true opportunity is when a company is conscientious about their reps and about the message of giving a chance to everyone.

-- Danny Richmond

Also, Check Out This Other Book Published by Success Publishing

Automatic Income Machines

Free Preview Bonus

Automatic Income Machines: e-Business Blueprint

With an economic whiplash that hits most the countries today; more people are joining ranks in achieving economic progress through the internet. The internet world had become an American Dream while others look at it as the other side of the world with the greener pasture.

Many had indeed taken their chance in starting an online business, yet not all are ready to face all the challenges and the complexities of surviving in the internet business arena.

However, for those who were lucky enough to survive, they lived to testify to the kind of life online business offers.

This "e-Business Blueprint" aims to provide beginners with a guide on setting up an online business and guiding you through the simple steps to achieve success.

With proper knowledge and determination, success on any online business can be achievable and in fact, rewarding. It's just a matter of planning and driving you towards a goal that can really make your dream comes true.

CHAPTER 1: Reasons for Getting Into an Online Business

People got different reasons for going into online business. But most often, online business is for people who got tired of working 8-5 or 9-6 every day. Rushing each morning for a gulp of coffee before fighting his way through traffic and hoping he could be earlier than usual!

As you realized that you are getting tired of working for someone else and you want to become your own boss, you start thinking of the possibility to make it big in the internet business. Hoping, you are right, and then the best way to set up a business with a greater chance to make it to success is to start now!

Here are just a few of the many reasons why you must start with your internet business.

Goodbye to Traffic and Early Morning Rush

With an internet business, you don't need to rush up too early that you need to skip eating breakfast just so you can arrive in time for work. But when you are living in an overcrowded metropolis where you had to go through jam-packed traffic, stress and anxiety can be a daily part of your routine!

Online business can help you save a lot of money by not traveling every day. Count the savings you can have when you don't need to go out for work. You can likewise save your time and convert the time spent for daily trips into more productive inputs.

No Need Putting Up with a Toxic Boss

Most often people got fed up and want to get out of their work because they have a toxic person for a boss. Most often, bosses thought that their employees are there to please them all the time. This often happens when you are working in a sole proprietorship type of business or a one-man organization. Most often than not, you feed to your boss whims and schemes rather than get productive in your tasks. In the end, you feel thoroughly burnt out and find a quick way to change job.

Working at your own Pace and Time

When you are running an online business, you can be your own boss. You can work at a chosen time and place. You can even have more time to yourself and to your family. However, this can have its own drawback. So, before you get out of your work, be sure your finances or the lack of will not cripple you. Proper timing is needed so your family will not suffer from your decision.

When you are free to decide for yourself whether you are going to work or not, be sure you manage your time effectively and efficiently. When you're alone to manage your time and no one is around to put pressure on you, you don't give yourself a reason to procrastinate. You need to learn to balance everything even without someone to answer to. Remember that every minute wasted is an opportunity lost in online business.

Unlimited Income Potential

Working on a regular career means putting up a cap on how much you can earn. But with online business, your ability to earn depends on how much time you want to put into your business. You can earn as much or as little as you want. The market for online business is too vast. You just learn to tap its unlimited resources and you go as far as you can.

You can target people around the world as the global market is getting bigger and bigger and more people are learning how to access the internet every day. You can work as much or as little as you choose. The marketplace for internet businesses is worldwide.

Per the later report of the Statistics portal, the number of internet users had risen up to 3.17 billion this year from 2.94 of the previous year. Doesn't that market large enough to dip your toes into?

Minimal Expenses for an Office

Since you are working from the comfort of your home, you don't need to rent an office space. You will again be saving a lot on your administrative expenses compared if you are running a conventional type of business.

In setting up your business, all you need to have is your laptop or PC and low-cost hardware and software which you can even get for free online if you're just diligent enough to browse through your internet.

Bigger Chance to Achieve more for Less Work

An online business allows you to work fewer hours and achieve more. There are some business models that can be fully automated. You just must set them up and (lo!), they can run on their own and earns you a passive income. This automation process now is widely used in the internet market. If you can't run your business on 100% automation, you can at least have it automated at 50% or more, so you can have more time for additional business to carry on.

What makes an online business unique than conventional ones is you can operate multiple businesses single-handedly. To simplify, you are operating a business that is almost next to impossible – Less capital, less time, and less effort for unlimited income streams potentials.

Common Problems you will Encounter at the Start of your Online Business

Starting your online business can be both rewarding and stimulating. However, you are sure to encounter a few problems that new entrepreneurs usually encounter. To steer clear of these issues, you must be aware of them and avoid them as they come along.

Tempting Opportunities and Resources

As you start hanging on the internet, you will be meeting a lot of opportunities along with remarkable resources to promising you great support in your online business. These products, usually software or a business opportunity, may be as great as their vendor advertise them. Nonetheless, if you jump from one opportunity to another, you will be losing your focus on your core business. It is, therefore, important that you start an online business with only what you absolutely need and have it run smoothly before getting into another. The same works with your software or any other tool.

Neglecting New Opportunities

Basically, this is the exact opposite of grabbing every opportunity that comes along. If you refuse to examine or look at any new opportunity sent your way because you have your focus set up trying to achieve a goal with a method that simply don't work, avoid overlooking the warning signs that tell you that you need to move on or move in another direction.

Doing Everything by Yourself

When you think it's better to keep all the profit, you keep trying to do everything so you can keep the money to yourself. Saving is always good for your business, but as your business develops, it will become impossible for you to embrace all the tasks. This is the time when you need to develop some way to ease up your workload. An example of these if subscribing for an auto responder that will take care of your mailing activities. Instead of manually sending letters, answering queries, the auto-responder allows you to maintain and develop relationships with your customer base and up-sell or cross-sell your products and services.

Having Too Many Choices

Affiliate marketing is a good start for an online business for you can earn as soon as someone buys from your inks. This is the reason why it is so popular with many people. Affiliate marketing method has many positive aspects but there are too many choices that it is confusing to know which to promote. Before you jump into marketing a new software by way of an affiliate program, check how much commission you can earn from it, how you can get paid, and know if there is some support you can get from the owner. It is also important to know if the product sells before promoting it.

The Internet is Bigger than What You Think

Having an online business doesn't mean that people will naturally visit your website and buy things that you offer. The internet is such an enormous marketplace that you need to know how to get prospective customers to visit your visit so you can have the chance to convert these visits into sales. Meaning, you need to learn how to generate website traffic by utilizing both free and paid traffic generators.

No Support from Family and Friend

Sometimes, we presume that our family and friends will be our loyal customer. Sad to say, in most cases, it doesn't usually happen especially during the start of your business. There are even cases when they will discourage you from doing online business. Though these people mean well, don't get easily swayed and let your goals and efforts get destructed. If you have set your goal and created a business plan to back it up, you have every opportunity to get successful.

Regardless of whom you are, your age, gender, technical skills, educational background, you can always start your own internet business. You can always harness whatever skill you have through various learning platforms and resources provided on the internet for a certain fee or for free.

DOWNLOAD Automatic Income Machines NOW!

www.ingramcontent.com/pod-product-compliance
Lightning Source LLC
Chambersburg PA
CBHW081317180526
45170CB00007B/2748